Believe in Love

~~~

INSPIRING WORDS
FROM
Pope Francis

~~~

POPE FRANCIS
EDITED BY ALICIA VON STAMWITZ

Cincinnati, Ohio

Believe in Love is published in collaboration with the Libreria Editrice Vaticana. All excerpts © 2014–2018 Libreria Editrice Vaticana and used by permission. Jorge Bergolio's Personal Credo reprinted from Austen Ivereigh, *The Great Reformer* (New York: Henry Holt, 2014), 100–101. Used with permission.

Cover and book design by Mark Sullivan
Cover image © Giampiero Sposito | Reuters

LIBRARY OF CONGRESS CATALOGING-IN-PUBLICATION DATA
Names: Francis, Pope, 1936- author. | Stamwitz, Alicia von, editor.
Title: Believe in love : inspiring words from Pope Francis / Pope Francis ; edited by Alicia von Stamwitz.
Description: Cincinnati : Franciscan Media, 2018.
Identifiers: LCCN 2018028244 | ISBN 9781632532572 (trade paper)
Subjects: LCSH: Love--Religious aspects--Catholic Church. | Catholic Church--Doctrines.
Classification: LCC BV4639 .F6613 2018 | DDC 241/.4--dc23
LC record available at https://lccn.loc.gov/2018028244

ISBN 978-1-63253-257-2

Published by Franciscan Media
28 W. Liberty St.
Cincinnati, OH 45202
www.FranciscanMedia.org

Printed in the United States of America.
Printed on acid-free paper.
18 19 20 21 22 5 4 3 2 1

Contents

Introduction

> The heart of the human being aspires to great things, lofty values, deep friendships, ties that are strengthened rather than broken by the trials of life. The human being aspires to love and to be loved. This is our deepest aspiration: to love and be loved; and definitively.
>
> — Pope Francis, July 5, 2014

Long before Jorge Bergoglio was elected to the papacy, he was an ordinary person trying to live a Christian life in a complex world. He was the eldest of five children, born to first-generation Italian immigrants in Argentina. He played soccer and basketball, liked to dance, cook, and play the piano, and had a lively sense of humor. Before joining the Jesuits, he worked as a janitor at a stocking factory and studied chemistry. Early in his seminary days, he was love-struck by a young woman he met at a family wedding. Her beauty and intellectual radiance dazzled him and left him sleepless for a week.

In the end, as we know, Jorge chose religious life over marriage. But his rich and varied life experience has served him well as pope. When he speaks about the universal human desire "to love and be loved," listeners sense a genuine understanding of human nature. His voice rises with excitement. He becomes animated, and a world of emotions plays across his face. Joy. Tenderness. Hope. Rage against hatred and injustice. Delight in kindness and goodness. Confidence that "all will be well," because God's love will triumph in the end.

A few weeks before his thirty-third birthday, on an eight-day retreat to prepare for his ordination, Jorge wrote a short "Credo," or statement of his personal beliefs (see Appendix). This credo is the springboard for the quotes gathered in this new collection of Pope Francis's written and spoken words since his election in March 2013. Here are his most intimate thoughts about the purpose and promise of love, "the greatest power for the transformation of reality."

Although the chapters and quotations have been arranged in a certain way, they may be read in any order. Let your experience and curiosity be your guide. Trust your instincts, trust yourself, and trust that the message you most need to hear will find you. Whether you are at the beginning, middle, or end of your spiritual journey, may Pope Francis's words open your eyes to true love: the kind of love that will never end.

—*Alicia von Stamwitz, editor*

Chapter One

~ I believe in love, and I want to love a lot ~

GOD CALLS YOU BY NAME

God calls each one of you by name. All of you are the "you" of God, precious in his eyes, worthy of respect and loved (cf. Isaiah 43:4). Welcome with joy this dialogue that God offers you, this appeal he makes to you, calling you by name.

MESSAGE TO YOUTH,
FEBRUARY 11, 2018

COME!—WHO?—YOU!

In today's Gospel, Jesus says: "Come to me, all who labor and are heavy laden, and I will give you rest" (Matthew 11:28). The Lord knows how arduous life can be. He knows that many things weary the heart: disappointments and wounds of the past, burdens to carry and wrongs to bear in the present, uncertainties and worries about the future.

In the face of all this, Jesus's first word is an invitation, a call to move and respond: "Come."

The mistake, when things go wrong, is to stay where we are, lying there. It seems obvious, but how difficult it is to respond and open ourselves! It is not easy. In dark times it feels natural to keep to ourselves, to ruminate over how unfair life is, over how ungrateful others are, how mean the world is, and so on. We all know it. We have had this awful experience a few times. But in this way, locked up inside ourselves, we see everything as grim. Then we even grow accustomed to sadness, which becomes like home: that sadness overcomes us; this sadness is a terrible thing. Jesus, however, wants to pull us out of this "quicksand" and thus says to each one: "Come!—Who?—You, you, you." The way out is in connecting, in extending a hand and lifting our gaze to those who truly love us.

ANGELUS,
JULY 9, 2017

GOD TAKES THE FIRST STEP

The first step that God takes toward us is that of a love that anticipates and is unconditional. God is the first to love. God does not love because there is something in us that engenders love. God loves us because he himself is love, and, by its very nature, love tends to spread and give itself. God does not even condition his benevolence on our conversion. If anything, this is a consequence of God's love.

GENERAL AUDIENCE,
JUNE 14, 2017

REPEAT IT: I AM SURE THAT GOD LOVES ME

It is easy to say: God loves us. We all say it. But think a bit. Each one of us is able to ask: Am I sure that God loves me? It is not so easy to say it. But it is true. This is a good exercise, to say to oneself: God loves me. This is the root of our certainty, the root of hope. The Lord has abundantly poured into our hearts the Spirit—which is the love of God—as artisan, as guarantor, precisely so that he may nourish the faith within us and keep this hope alive. This is a certainty: God loves me. "But in this difficult moment?"—God loves me. "I, who have done this bad and cruel thing?"—God loves me. No one can take this certainty away. We must repeat it as a prayer: God loves me. I am sure that God loves me. I am sure that God loves me.

GENERAL AUDIENCE,
FEBRUARY 15, 2017

GOD'S DREAM FOR US

We were created to love and to be loved. God, who is Love, created us to make us participants in his life, to be loved by him and to love him, and with him, to love all other people. This is God's "dream" for mankind.

ANGELUS,
OCTOBER 29, 2017

GOD INVITES US

What is it that draws God? It is love for us: we are his children, he loves us and wants to free us from evil, from sickness, from death, and to bring us to his home, to his Kingdom....

And from us too there arises a love, a desire: the good always draws us, truth draws us, life, happiness, beauty attracts us.... Jesus is the meeting point of this mutual attraction, of this double movement. He is God and man: Jesus. God and man. But who took the initiative? God, always! God's love always comes before our own! He always takes the initiative. He waits for us, he invites us, the initiative is always his.

ANGELUS,
JANUARY 6, 2014

DON'T PUT ON ANY MAKE-UP

Jesus wants us as we are, just as he wanted his friends, with their defects, desiring to correct them yes, but as they were, that's how the Lord loves you. Don't put on any make-up, don't put any make-up on the heart, but show yourself to Jesus as you are so that he can help you to move forward in life. When Jesus looks at us, he does not think about how perfect we are, but about all the love we have in our hearts to give him and to follow him. That is the important thing for him, that is the greatest thing.

ANGELUS,
JANUARY 21, 2018

LOVE WHEREVER YOU FIND YOURSELF

To be holy does not require being a bishop, a priest, or a religious. We are frequently tempted to think that holiness is only for those who can withdraw from ordinary affairs to spend much time in prayer. That is not the case. We are all called to be holy by living our lives with love and by bearing witness in everything we do, wherever we find ourselves. Are you called to the consecrated life? Be holy by living out your commitment with joy. Are you married? Be holy by loving and caring for your husband or wife, as Christ does for the Church. Do you work for a living? Be holy by laboring with integrity and skill in the service of your brothers and sisters. Are you a parent or grandparent? Be holy by patiently teaching the little ones how to follow Jesus. Are you in a position of authority? Be holy by working for the common good and renouncing personal gain.

GAUDETE ET EXSULTATE, 14

TRUE LOVE

How truly difficult it is to let ourselves be loved! We would always like a part of us to be freed of the debt of gratitude, while in reality we are completely indebted, because God loved us first and, with love, he saves us completely.

Let us now ask the Lord for the grace to know the greatness of his love, which wipes away our every sin.

Let us allow ourselves to be purified by love, in order to recognize true love!

HOMILY,
MARCH 9, 2018

THE POWER OF A CHANGED HEART

Love is the greatest power for the transformation of reality because it pulls down the walls of selfishness and fills the ditches that keep us apart. This is the love that comes from a changed heart, from a heart of stone that has been turned into a heart of flesh, a human heart. And this is what grace does, the grace of Jesus Christ which we have all received.

ADDRESS,
JUNE 17, 2013

A MOTHER'S LOVE

As a mother takes upon herself the burdens and weariness of her children, so too does God take upon himself our sins and troubles. He who knows us and loves us infinitely, is mindful of our prayers and wipes away our tears. As he looks at us, he is always moved and becomes tender-hearted, with a love from the depths of his being, for beyond any evil we are capable of, we always remain his children; he wants to take us in his arms, protect us, and free us from harm and evil. Let us allow these words of the Lord to resound in our hearts: "As a mother comforts, so will I comfort you."

The consolation we need, amid the turmoil we experience in life, is precisely the presence of God in our hearts.

HOMILY,
OCTOBER 1, 2016

AN INFINITE LOVE

Love of God is always greater than anything we can imagine; it even reaches beyond any sin with which our conscience may charge us. His is an infinite love, one that knows no bounds. It is free of all those obstacles that we, for our part, tend to set in front of others, out of fear that they may strip us of our freedom.... The words of the apostle [John] are a reassuring confirmation that our hearts should trust, always and unhesitatingly, in the Father's love: "No matter what our hearts may charge us with, God is greater than our hearts" (1 John 3:20).

HOMILY,
MARCH 9, 2018

THE ROCK OF TRUE LOVE

What do we mean by *love*? Is it only a feeling, a psychophysical state? Certainly, if that is it, then we cannot build on anything solid. But if instead love is a relationship, then it is a reality that grows, and we can also say by way of example that it is built up like a home. And a home is built together, not alone!...

Living together is an art—a patient, beautiful, fascinating journey. It does not end once you have won each other's love.... Rather, it is precisely there where it begins!

ADDRESS TO ENGAGED COUPLES,
FEBRUARY 14, 2014

LOVE FILLS THE VOID

Only love fills the void, the negative chasms that evil opens in hearts and in history. Only love can do this, and this is God's joy!...

If in our heart there is no mercy, no joy of forgiveness, we are not in communion with God, even if we observe all of his precepts, for it is love that saves, not the practice of precepts alone. It is love of God and neighbor that brings fulfilment to all the commandments.

ANGELUS,
SEPTEMBER 15, 2013

GOD IS OUR REFUGE

God is not a distant and anonymous being: he is our refuge, the wellspring of our peace and tranquility. He is the rock of our salvation, to which we can cling with the certainty of not falling; one who clings to God never falls! He is our defense against the evil which is ever lurking. God is a great friend, ally, father to us, but we do not always realize it. We do not realize that we have a friend, an ally, a father who loves us.

ANGELUS,
FEBRUARY 26, 2017

LET GOD'S LOVE WARM YOU

Let me ask you: Are there moments when you place yourself quietly in the Lord's presence, when you calmly spend time with him, when you bask in his gaze? Do you let his fire inflame your heart? Unless you let him warm you more and more with his love and tenderness, you will not catch fire.

GAUDETE ET EXSULTATE, 151

OUR GOD IS REAL

Let us recognize that God is not something vague, our God is not a God "spray," he is tangible; he is not abstract but has a name: "God is love." His is not a sentimental, emotional kind of love but the love of the Father who is the origin of all life, the love of the Son who dies on the cross and is raised, the love of the Spirit who renews human beings and the world. Thinking that God is love does us so much good, because it teaches us to love, to give ourselves to others as Jesus gave himself to us and walks with us.

ANGELUS,
MAY 26, 2013

GOD WILL COMFORT YOU

How often do I think that we are afraid of the tenderness of God and because we are afraid of God's tenderness, we do not allow it to be felt within us.... The Heart of Christ is the tenderness of God. "How could I fail you? How could I abandon you? When you are alone, disoriented, lost, come to me, and I will save you, I will comfort you."

HOMILY,
JUNE 12, 2015

GOD'S LOVE REACHES EVERYWHERE

I thank you and I would like to take advantage of this meeting with you, who work in the prisons throughout Italy, to send my greetings to all the inmates. Please tell them that I am praying for them, I have them at heart, I am praying to the Lord and to Our Lady that they may be able to get through this difficult period in their lives in a positive way, that they may not become discouraged or close in on themselves. You know how one day things go well, but the next day they feel discouraged, and this fluctuation is difficult. The Lord is close, but tell them with your actions, with your words and with your hearts, that the Lord does not remain outside, he does not remain outside their cells, he does not remain outside the prison; rather, he is inside, he is there. You can say this: the Lord is inside with them; he too is a prisoner; even today, he is imprisoned by our egoism, by our systems, by so many injustices, for it is easy to punish the weakest while the big fish swim freely in the sea. No cell is so isolated that it is shut to the Lord, none. He is there, he weeps with them, he works with them, he hopes with them, his paternal and maternal love reaches everywhere.

ADDRESS TO PRISON CHAPLAINS,
OCTOBER 23, 2013

LOVE IS GOD'S YES

The love of God is his "yes" to all creation and at the heart of this is man. It is God's "yes" to the union between man and woman, in openness and service to life in all its phases; it is God's "yes" and his commitment to a humanity that is often wounded, mistreated and dominated by a lack of love.

LETTER TO FAMILIES,
MARCH 25, 2017

LOVE FREELY GIVEN

None of us can live without love. And a bad form of slavery to which we can all fall victim is that of thinking that love must be earned. Perhaps a good part of contemporary man's anguish comes from this: believing that, if we are not strong, attractive and beautiful, no one will take care of us. Many people nowadays seek visibility only to fill an interior void, as though we were always in need of approval. However, can you imagine a world in which everyone is looking for ways to attract the attention of others, and in which no one is instead willing to freely give love to another person? Imagine a world like this: a world without freely given love! It appears to be a human world but in reality it is hellish. Much of mankind's narcissism conceals a feeling of loneliness and orphanhood. Behind many forms of behavior that seem to be unexplainable there lies a question: is it possible that I do not deserve to be called by name, that is, to be loved? Because love always calls [us] by name.

ANGELUS,
JANUARY 6, 2014

WE ARE BEAUTIFUL TO GOD

Is it possible that God has some children whom he does not love? No. We are all God's beloved children.... There is Someone who has impressed within us a primordial beauty, which no sin, no bad choice, can ever completely erase. In the eyes of God, we are always small fountains made to gush forth good water. Jesus says to the Samaritan woman: "the water that I shall give [you] will become in [you] a spring of water welling up to eternal life" (John 4:14).

GENERAL AUDIENCE,
JUNE 14, 2017

THE LORD IS WAITING FOR YOU

I would like to say—sincerely—I would like to say to those who feel far from God and from the Church—I would like to say respectively—to all those who are fearful or indifferent: the Lord is also calling you to be a part of his people and he does so with deep respect and love! The Lord is calling you. The Lord is seeking you. The Lord is waiting for you. The Lord does not proselytize, he loves, and this love seeks you, waits for you, you who at this moment do not believe or are far away. And this is the love of God.

ANGELUS,
JANUARY 6, 2014

CHAPTER TWO

~ I believe in the goodness of others, and I want to love others without fear ~

OUR ROYAL ROAD

As Christians, we are bound above all to practice the Lord's command: "Just as I have loved you, you also should love one another. By this everyone will know that you are my disciples" (John 13:34–35). The love of God, made incarnate in life, is thus our royal road, and the basis of our common responsibility before the world to account for the hope that is in us (cf. 1 Peter 3:15).

ADDRESS,
DECEMBER 7, 2017

REACH OUT IN FRIENDSHIP

No matter how much or how little we have individually, each one of us is called to personally reach out and serve our brothers and sisters in need. There is always someone near us who is in need, materially, emotionally, spiritually. The greatest gift we can give to them is our friendship, our concern, our tenderness, our love for Jesus.

ADDRESS TO YOUNG PEOPLE,
JANUARY 18, 2015

LOVE IS THE BEST MEDICINE

What medicine is needed in order to change the heart of an unhappy person? What medicine can change the heart of a person who is not happy? [they reply: "love!"] Louder! [they shout: "love!"] Good! Very good, well done everyone! And how do we make the person feel that we love them? We must first embrace them. Make them feel wanted, which is important, and they will stop being sad. Love calls for love in a stronger way than hatred calls for death.... A wind of liberation blows here on our faces. Here, the gift of hope is sprouting up. And the hope is that of God the Father who loves us as we are: he loves us all and always. Thank you!

GENERAL AUDIENCE,
JUNE 14, 2017

GOD SENDS US TO EVERYONE

Where does Jesus send us? There are no borders, no limits: he sends us to everyone. The Gospel is for everyone, not just for some. It is not only for those who seem closer to us, more receptive, and more welcoming. It is for everyone. Do not be afraid to go and to bring Christ into every area of life, to the fringes of society, even to those who seem farthest away or most indifferent. The Lord seeks all, he wants everyone to feel the warmth of his mercy and his love.

PRAYER VIGIL, WORLD YOUTH DAY,
JULY 27, 2013

A PRAYER INSPIRED BY ST. FRANCIS OF ASSISI

Lord, make us instruments of your peace.
Help us to recognize the evil latent in a communication that does not build communion.
Help us to remove the venom from our judgments.
Help us to speak about others as our brothers and sisters.
You are faithful and trustworthy; may our words be seeds of goodness for the world:
where there is shouting, let us practice listening;
where there is confusion, let us inspire harmony;
where there is ambiguity, let us bring clarity;
where there is exclusion, let us offer solidarity;
where there is sensationalism, let us use sobriety;
where there is superficiality, let us raise real questions;
where there is prejudice, let us awaken trust;
where there is hostility, let us bring respect;
where there is falsehood, let us bring truth.
Amen.

MESSAGE FOR WORLD COMMUNICATIONS DAY,
JANUARY 24, 2018

REDISCOVER THE JOY OF GIVING

To do good without counting the cost, even when unasked, even when you gain nothing thereby, even if it is unpleasant. That is what God wants. He, who became small for our sake, asks us to offer something for the least of his brothers and sisters. Who are they? They are those who have nothing to give in return, the needy, the hungry, the stranger, the prisoner, the poor (cf. Mt 25:31–46). We give a gift pleasing to Jesus when we care for a sick person, spend time with a difficult person, help someone for the sake of helping, or forgive someone who has hurt us. These are gifts freely given, and they cannot be lacking in the lives of Christians. Jesus reminds us that if we only love those who love us, we do as the pagans do (cf. Mt 5:46–47). Today let us look at our hands, so often empty of love, and let us try to think of some free gift that we can give without expecting anything in return.

HOMILY,
JANUARY 6, 2018

BEGIN ANEW EVERY DAY

Even for a Christian, knowing how to love is never a thing acquired once and for all. We must begin anew every day. We must practice it so that our love for the brothers and sisters we encounter may become mature and purified from those limitations or sins that render it incomplete, egotistical, sterile, and unfaithful. We have to learn the art of loving every day. Listen to this: every day we must learn the art of loving; every day we must patiently follow the school of Christ.

REGINA COELI,
MAY 21, 2017

LEARN TO SAY, "I'M SORRY"

In life we err frequently, we make many mistakes. We all do.... We accuse the other to avoid saying "I'm sorry," or "Forgive me." It's an old story! It is an instinct that stands at the origin of so many disasters.

Let us learn to acknowledge our mistakes and to ask for forgiveness: "Forgive me if today I raised my voice." "I'm sorry if I passed without greeting you." "Excuse me if I was late...if this week I was very silent...if I spoke too much without ever listening." "Excuse me; I forgot." "I'm sorry I was angry and I took it out on you."... Don't let a day end without asking forgiveness, without peace returning to our home, to our family.

ADDRESS TO ENGAGED COUPLES,
FEBRUARY 14, 2014

BE PROPHETS OF GOODNESS AND TRUTH

You are artisans of the future. Why? First, because inside you, you have three desires: the desire for beauty. You like beauty and when you make music, produce theater, and paint—beautiful things—you are looking for beauty, you are searching for beauty. Now secondly: You are prophets of goodness. You like goodness and being good. And this goodness is contagious, it helps everyone else. And now third: you thirst for the truth....

These three desires that you have in your heart, you must carry forward to the future and make the future beautiful with goodness and truth. Have you understood? This is a challenge; it is your challenge.... You can do this, you have the power to do it.

ADDRESS TO YOUTH,
AUGUST 28, 2013

THE PATH OF LOVE

Jesus shows us the path to follow Him: the path of love....

It is a real path, a path that leads us to come out of ourselves and go towards others. Jesus showed us that the love of God is realized in love for our neighbor. Both go hand-in-hand. The pages of the Gospel are full of this love: adults and children, educated and uneducated, rich and poor, just and sinners all were welcomed into the heart of Christ.

REGINA COELI,
MAY 10, 2015

DO NOT BE AFRAID TO LOVE OTHERS

The only thing that Jesus asks for: to be made welcome. Let us think of all who live in desperation because they have never met anyone who showed them attention or comforted them, anyone who made them feel precious and important. Can we, disciples of the Crucified One, refuse to go to those places where no one wants to go, for fear of compromising ourselves or of the opinion of others, and hence deny these brethren of ours the proclamation of God's word?…

Do not be afraid, do not be afraid. Do not be afraid of love, of the love of God our Father. Do not be afraid. Do not be afraid to receive the grace of Jesus Christ, do not be afraid of our freedom which is given by the grace of Jesus Christ or, as Paul used to say: "you are not under law but under grace." Do not be afraid of grace, do not be afraid of going out of our Christian communities to seek and find the ninety-nine who are not at home. And go and talk to them, and tell them what we think, go and show them our love, which is the love of God.

ADDRESS,
JUNE 17, 2013

LET US BE INFECTED BY GOODNESS

In the face of a poor or sick person, we must not be afraid to look him in the eye and to draw near with tenderness and compassion, and to touch him and embrace him. I have often asked this of people who help others, to do so looking them in the eye, not to be afraid to touch them; that this gesture of help may also be a gesture of communication: We too need to be welcomed by them. A gesture of tenderness, a gesture of compassion.... Let us ask you: when you help others, do you look them in the eye? Do you embrace them without being afraid to touch them? Do you embrace them with tenderness? Think about this: How do you help? From a distance or with tenderness, with closeness? If evil is contagious, so is goodness. Therefore, there needs to be ever more abundant goodness in us. Let us be infected by goodness and let us spread goodness!

ANGELUS,
FEBRUARY 15, 2015

THE YARDSTICK IS LOVE

Mercy is the heart of God. It must also be the heart of the members of the one great family of his children: a heart which beats all the more strongly wherever human dignity—as a reflection of the face of God in his creatures—is in play. Jesus tells us that love for others—foreigners, the sick, prisoners, the homeless, even our enemies—is the yardstick by which God will judge our actions. Our eternal destiny depends on this. It is not surprising that the apostle Paul tells the Christians of Rome to rejoice with those who rejoice and to weep with those who weep (cf. Romans 12:15), or that he encourages the Corinthians to take up collections as a sign of solidarity with the suffering members of the Church (cf. 1 Corinthians 16:2-3). And St. John writes: "If anyone has the world's goods and sees his brother or sister in need, yet refuses help, how does God's love abide in him?" (1 John 3:17; cf. James 2:15–16).

MESSAGE FOR WORLD DAY OF PEACE,
JANUARY 1, 2016

A SMILE OPENS THE DOORS OF HEARTS

There are no bad children just as there are no adolescents who are entirely evil, but unhappy people do exist. And what can make us feel happy if not the experience of giving and receiving love? The life of human beings is an exchange of glances: someone who, by looking at us, steals a first smile. Thus, we who smile freely at those who are locked up in sadness, open a way out for them: an exchange of glances, looking people in the eye will open the doors of hearts.

ANGELUS,
JANUARY 6, 2014

THE GREATEST COMMANDMENT

This Sunday, the liturgy presents us with a brief, but very important Gospel passage (Matthew 22:34–40). Matthew the Evangelist recounts that the Pharisees assemble in order to put Jesus to the test. One of them, a doctor of the Law, asks him this question: "Teacher, which one is the great commandment in the law?" (22:36). It is an insidious question, because more than 600 precepts are mentioned in the Law of Moses. How should the great commandment be distinguished among these? But Jesus responds without hesitation: "You shall love the Lord your God with all your heart and with all your soul and with all your mind." And he adds: "You shall love your neighbor as yourself" (vv. 37, 39).

This response of Jesus is not to be taken for granted, because, among the numerous precepts of the Hebrew Law, the most important were the Ten Commandments, communicated directly by God to Moses, as the conditions of the covenant with the people. But Jesus wants to make it understood that without love for God and for our neighbor there is no true fidelity to this covenant with the Lord. You may do many good things, fulfil many precepts, many good things, but if you do not have love, this serves no purpose.

ANGELUS,
OCTOBER 29, 2017

WE ARE ALL BROTHERS AND SISTERS

I want to tell you that I read what the children wrote here [on posters]: "peace," "forgiveness," "unity," and so many things…"love." We must work and pray and do everything possible for peace. But without love, without friendship, without tolerance, without forgiveness, peace is not possible. Each one of us must do something. I wish peace to you, to you and to all Central Africans, great peace among you. That you may live in peace in whatever place, ethnicity, culture, religion or social status. Everyone in peace! Everyone! Because we are all brothers and sisters.

GREETING TO REFUGEES,
NOVEMBER 29, 2015

SHOUT WITH YOUR HEARTS!

Do not be afraid to make a ruckus, to ask questions that make people think! And don't worry if sometimes you feel that you are few and far between. The Gospel always grows from small beginnings. So make yourselves heard. I want you to shout! But not with your voices. No! I want you to shout with your lives, with your hearts, and in this way to be signs of hope to those who need encouragement, a helping hand to the sick, a welcoming smile to the stranger, a kindly support to the lonely.

HOMILY,
NOVEMBER 30, 2017

TWO DIMENSIONS OF LOVE

What is love? "Is it a soap opera, Father? What we see on TV programs?" Some think that that is love. It is so good to speak of love, very beautiful, beautiful, beautiful things can be said. However, love has two axes on which it pivots, and if a person, a young person doesn't have these two axes—these two dimensions of love—it's not love. First of all, love is more in works than in words: love is concrete....

And the second dimension, the second axis on which love pivots, is that love is always communicated, that is, love listens and responds, love is built in dialogue, in communion: it is communicated. Love is neither deaf nor mute, it communicates. These two dimensions are very useful to understand what love is, which is not a romantic sentiment of the moment or a story, no. It's concrete, it's in deeds. And it is communicated, that is, it is always in dialogue.

ADDRESS TO CHILDREN AND YOUNG PEOPLE, JUNE 21, 2015

WITHOUT LOVE, LIFE IS STERILE

It is confirmed by another text in the Book of Exodus, the so-called "Covenant Code," where it is said that one cannot adhere to the covenant with the Lord and mistreat those who enjoy his protection. And who are those who enjoy his protection? The Bible says: the widow, the orphan and the stranger, the migrant, that is, the most lonely and defenseless people (cf. Exodus 22:20–21). In responding to those Pharisees who question him, Jesus also tries to help them put their religiosity in order, to distinguish what truly matters from what is less important. Jesus says: "On these two commandments depend all the law and the prophets" (Matthew 22:40). They are the most important, and the others depend on these two. And Jesus lived his life precisely in this way: preaching and practicing what truly matters and is essential, namely, love. Love gives impulse and fruitfulness to life and to the journey of life: without love, both life and faith remain sterile.

ANGELUS,
OCTOBER 29, 2017

TENDERNESS PASSES FROM HEART TO HANDS

Do not forget the "medicine of caresses": it is so important! A caress, a smile, is full of meaning for the sick person. It is a simple gesture, but it lifts one up; a person feels supported, feels healing is near, feels as a person, not a number. Do not forget it.... Remember how Jesus touched the leper: not in a distracted, indifferent, or annoyed manner, but attentive and loving, so it makes him or her feel respected and taken care of. In doing so, the contact that you establish with patients accompanies them as an echo of God the Father's closeness, of his tenderness for each one of his children. Precisely tenderness: tenderness is the key to understanding the sick. The sick cannot be understood with harshness. Tenderness is the key to understanding them, and is also a precious medicine for their healing. And tenderness passes from the heart to the hands; it passes, with full respect and love, through the "touching" of wounds.

ADDRESS TO NURSING PROFESSIONALS,
MARCH 3, 2018

A LOVE FREE FROM SELFISHNESS

The Word of God calls us to love one another, even if we do not always understand each other, and do not always get along…it is then that Christian love is seen. A love which manifests even if there are differences of opinion or character. Love is greater than these differences! This is the love that Jesus taught us. It is a new love because Jesus and his Spirit renewed it. It is a redeeming love, free from selfishness.

REGINA COELI,
MAY 10, 2015

BRING GOD'S LOVE AND GOODNESS TO ALL!

Dear families, dear brothers and sisters, I encourage you to carry the Gospel of Jesus Christ everywhere, even to those most de-Christianized, especially in the margins of life. Evangelize with love, bring God's love to all. Tell all those you meet on the streets of your mission that God loves man as he is, even with his limitations, with his mistakes, even with his sins. That is why he sent his Son, that he might take our sins onto himself. May you be messengers and witnesses of the infinite goodness and inexhaustible mercy of the Father.

ADDRESS,
FEBRUARY 1, 2014

CHAPTER THREE

~ I believe in God's patience, as good and as welcoming as a summer's night ~

LET US TRUST IN GOD'S PATIENCE

God is patient with us because he loves us, and those who love are able to understand, to hope, to inspire confidence; they do not give up, they do not burn bridges, they are able to forgive. Let us remember this in our lives as Christians: God always waits for us, even when we have left him behind! He is never far from us, and if we return to him, he is ready to embrace us….

In my own life, I have so often seen God's merciful countenance, his patience.

HOMILY,
APRIL 7, 2013

THIS IS HOW GOD LOVES US!

There is no person, as bad a life as he may have lived, who, faced with despair, is without recourse to grace. We all appear before God empty-handed, somewhat like the tax collector in the parable who had stopped to pray at the back of the Temple (cf. Luke 18:13). Each time a person, performing the last examination of conscience of his life, discovers that his shortcomings far exceed his good deeds, he must not feel discouraged, but must entrust himself to God's mercy. And this gives us hope; it opens our heart!

God is Father, and he awaits our return to the very end. And when the prodigal son returns and begins to confess his sins, the father closes his mouth with an embrace. (cf. Luke 15:20). This is God: this is how he loves us!

GENERAL AUDIENCE,
OCTOBER 25, 2017

AN OVERFLOWING LOVE

God's forgiveness is the symbol of his overflowing love for each of us. It is the love that leaves us free to distance ourselves, like the prodigal son, but which awaits our return every day. It is the resourceful love of the shepherd for the lost sheep. It is the tenderness which welcomes each sinner who knocks at his door. The Heavenly Father—our Father—is filled, is full of love and he wants to offer it to us.

ANGELUS,
SEPTEMBER 17, 2017

AN INFINITE LOVE

God so loves us that that he has made us his children, and, when we see him face-to-face, we will discover all the more the greatness of his love (cf. 1 John 3:1–10,19–22). Not only that. The love of God is always greater than anything we can imagine; it even reaches beyond any sin with which our conscience may charge us. His is an infinite love, one that knows no bounds.

HOMILY,
MARCH 9, 2018

GOD IS LIKE A MOTHER WITH HER BABY

As when a mother takes her child upon her knee and caresses him or her: so the Lord will do and does with us. This is the cascade of tenderness which gives us much consolation. "As one whom his mother comforts, so I will comfort you" (Isaiah 66:13). Every Christian, and especially you and I, is called to be a bearer of this message of hope that gives serenity and joy: God's consolation, his tenderness towards all. But if we first experience the joy of being consoled by him, of being loved by him, then we can bring that joy to others. This is important if our mission is to be fruitful: to feel God's consolation and to pass it on to others!... Do not be afraid, because the Lord is the Lord of consolation, he is the Lord of tenderness. The Lord is a Father and he says that he will be for us like a mother with her baby, with a mother's tenderness.

HOMILY,
JULY 7, 2013

GOD SEES THE SEEDS OF GOOD

At times we are in a great hurry to judge, to categorize, to put the good here, the bad there.... God, however, knows how to wait. With patience and mercy he gazes into the "field" of life of every person; he sees much better than we do the filth and the evil, but he also sees the seeds of good and waits with trust for them to grow. God is patient, he knows how to wait. This is so beautiful: our God is a patient father, who always waits for us and waits with his heart in hand to welcome us, to forgive us. He always forgives us if we go to him.

ANGELUS,
JULY 20, 2014

GOD DOES NOT GIVE UP ON US

Let us think back to that dark moment when the first crime of humanity was committed, when the hand of Cain, blinded by envy, killed his brother Abel (cf. Genesis 4:8). As a result, the unfolding of the centuries has been marked by violence, wars, hatred and oppression. But God, who placed a sense of expectation within man made in his image and likeness, was waiting. God was waiting. He waited for so long that perhaps at a certain point it seemed he should have given up. But he could not give up because he could not deny himself (cf. 2 Timothy 2:13). Therefore he continued to wait patiently in the face of the corruption of man and peoples. The patience of God. How difficult it is to comprehend this: God's patience toward us....

God does not know outbursts of anger or impatience; he is always there, like the father in the parable of the prodigal son, waiting to catch from afar a glimpse of the lost son as he returns; and every day, with patience. The patience of God.

HOMILY,
DECEMBER 24, 2014

NOBODY CAN TAKE AWAY GOD'S LOVE

We are children of God because of the love of the Father's heart; it does not depend on our merits or on our actions, so no one can take that away from us—no one—not even the devil! Nobody can take away this dignity. Jesus's words encourage us never to despair. I think of the moms and dads who worry when they see their children distance themselves, setting off on dangerous paths. I think of parish priests and catechists who sometimes wonder if their work was in vain. But I also think of those who are in prison, who feel their lives are over. I think of all those who have made mistakes and cannot manage to envision the future, of those who hunger for mercy and forgiveness and believe they don't deserve it.... In any situation of life, I must not forget that I will never cease to be a child of God, to be a son of the Father who loves me and waits for my return. Even in the worst situations of life, God waits for me, God wants to embrace me, God is expecting me.

GENERAL AUDIENCE,
MAY 11, 2016

IMITATE THE PATIENCE OF THE LORD

Although you know very well that, during the night, the evil one continues to sow weeds, imitate the patience of the Lord of the harvest and trust in the good quality of his grain. Learn from his patience and generosity. He takes his time, because his loving gaze sees far into the distance. If love grows weak, the heart becomes impatient, anxious to be busy about many things, hounded by the fear of failure. Believe above all in the smallness of God's seeds. Trust in the power hidden in his yeast. Let your hearts be drawn to the great beauty that leads us to sell everything we have, in order to possess that divine treasure.

ADDRESS,
SEPTEMBER 7, 2017

DIVE INTO THE SEA OF GOD'S BOUNDLESS LOVE

In the weakness and frailty of our lives, we can turn to God with the confidence of children and enter into communion with him. In the face of so many wounds that hurt us and could harden our hearts, we are called to dive into the sea of prayer, which is the sea of God's boundless love, to taste his tenderness.

HOMILY,
MARCH 5, 2014

GOD WAITS FOR YOU

The love of God precedes everything. God is always first. He arrives before us, he precedes us. The Prophet Isaiah, or Jeremiah, I don't remember, said that God is like an almond blossom, because it is the first tree to flower in spring, meaning that God always flowers before us. When we arrive he is waiting for us, he calls us, he makes us walk. Always anticipating us. And this is called love, because God always waits for us.

"But, Father, I don't believe this, because if you only knew, Father; my life was so horrible, how can I think that God is waiting for me?"

God is waiting for you. And if you were a great sinner, he is waiting for you even more and waiting for you with great love, because he is first.

GENERAL AUDIENCE,
JUNE 18, 2014

THE LORD CHOSE YOU

"The LORD set his love upon you and chose you" (Deuteronomy 7:7). God is bound to us, he chose us, and this bond is forever, not so much because we are faithful, but because the Lord is faithful and endures our faithlessness, our indolence, our lapses.... We can experience and savor the tenderness of this love at every stage of life: in times of joy and of sadness, in times of good health and of frailty and of sickness.

HOMILY,
JUNE 27, 2014

THE LOVE OF GOD NEVER LEAVES US

God is love. And we move toward the light to find the love of God. But is God's love within us, even in the dark moments? Is the love of God there, hidden away? Yes, always! The love of God never leaves us. It is always with us. Do we trust in this love?

ADDRESS TO CHILDREN,
MAY 31, 2014

GOD'S LOVE IS GREATER THAN EVERYTHING

The peace the Lord offers us and guarantees us is not to be understood as the absence of worry, of disappointment, of failure, of reasons for suffering. If it were so, supposing we had managed to be at peace, that moment would end quickly, and we would inevitably fall prey to unease. Instead, the peace that springs from faith is a gift: it is the grace of feeling that God loves us and that he is always beside us; he does not leave us on our own even for a moment of our life. This, as the apostle states, generates patience, because we know that, even at the hardest and most disturbing moment, the Lord's mercy and goodness are greater than everything, and nothing will tear us from his hands and from communion with him.

GENERAL AUDIENCE,
FEBRUARY 15, 2017

GOD NEVER CONDEMNS

Remember this! God judges us by loving us! If I embrace his love then I am saved, if I refuse it, then I am condemned, not by him, but my own self, because God never condemns, he only loves and saves.

WAY OF THE CROSS,
MARCH 29, 2013

GOD IS A PATIENT FATHER

God does not forget us; the Father never abandons us. He is a patient father, always waiting for us! He respects our freedom, but he remains faithful forever. And when we come back to him, he welcomes us like children into his house, for he never ceases, not for one instant, to wait for us with love. And his heart rejoices over every child who returns.

ANGELUS,
SEPTEMBER 15, 2013

THE STUPENDOUS MYSTERY OF GOD'S LOVE

Awareness of the marvels that the Lord has wrought for our salvation disposes our minds and hearts to an attitude of thanksgiving to God for all that he has given us, for all that he has accomplished for the good of his people and for the whole of humanity. This marks the beginning of our conversion: it is the grateful response to the stupendous mystery of God's love. When we see the love that God has for us, we feel the desire to draw close to him: this is conversion.

GENERAL AUDIENCE,
MARCH 5, 2014

THE STEADFAST LOVE OF GOD

To move forward and grow on the journey of life, we must not have fear; we must have faith.... We must not think that God is a cruel, hard and severe master who wishes to punish us. If this mistaken image of God is within us our life cannot be fruitful, because we will live in fear and this will not lead us to anything constructive. On the contrary, fear paralyzes us; it causes our self-destruction. We are called to reflect in order to discover what our idea of God really is. Already in the Old Testament he revealed himself as "a God merciful and gracious, slow to anger, and abounding in steadfast love and faithfulness" (Exodus 34:6). And Jesus always showed us that God is not a severe or intolerant master, but a father full of love, of tenderness, a father full of goodness. Therefore, we can and must have immense faith in him.

ANGELUS,
NOVEMBER 19, 2017

THE LOGIC OF THE FATHER'S LOVE

Jesus wants to open our hearts to the logic of the Father's love which is free and generous. It is about allowing oneself to be astonished and fascinated by the "thoughts" and the "ways" of God which, as the prophet Isaiah recalls, are not our thoughts and not our ways (cf. Isaiah 55:8). Human thoughts are often marked by selfishness and personal advantages, and our narrow and contorted paths are not comparable to the wide and straight streets of the Lord. He uses mercy—do not forget this: He uses mercy—he forgives broadly, is filled with generosity and kindness which he pours forth on each of us. He opens for everyone the boundless territory of his love and his grace, which alone can give the human heart the fullness of joy....

God excludes no one and wants each of us to achieve his or her fullness. This is the love of our God, of our God who is Father.

ANGELUS,
SEPTEMBER 24, 2017

GOD IS ALL LOVE, AND ONLY LOVE

When the [Hebrew] people break the covenant, God presents himself to Moses in the cloud in order to renew that pact, proclaiming his own name and its meaning. Thus he says: "the Lord, a merciful and gracious God, slow to anger and rich in kindness and fidelity" (Exodus 34:6). This name implies that God is not distant and closed within himself, but is Life which seeks to be communicated, is openness, is Love which redeems man of his infidelity. God is "merciful," "gracious," and "rich in charity" because he offers himself to us so as to fill the gap of our limitations and our shortcomings, to forgive our mistakes, to lead us back to the path of justice and truth.

ANGELUS,
JUNE 11, 2017

YOU ARE INVITED TO ENTER THIS LOVE STORY

My brothers and sisters, God does not avenge himself. God loves, he does not avenge himself. He waits for us to forgive us, to embrace us. Through the "rejected stones"—and Christ is the first stone that the builders rejected—through situations of weakness and sin, God continues to circulate "the new wine" of his vineyard, namely mercy. This is the new wine of the Lord's vineyard: mercy. There is only one obstacle to the tenacious and tender will of God: our arrogance and our conceit which at times also becomes violence!...

The Christian faith...is not so much the sum of precepts and moral norms but rather, it is first and foremost a proposal of love which God makes through Jesus and continues to make with mankind. It is an invitation to enter into this love story, by becoming a lively and open vine, rich in fruits and hope for everyone.

ANGELUS,
OCTOBER 8, 2017

LET US BE ENVELOPED BY GOD'S LOVE

Dear brothers and sisters, let us be enveloped by the mercy of God; let us trust in his patience, which always gives us more time. Let us find the courage to return to his house, to dwell in his loving wounds, allowing ourselves be loved by him and to encounter his mercy in the sacraments. We will feel his wonderful tenderness, we will feel his embrace, and we too will become more capable of mercy, patience, forgiveness and love.

HOMILY,
APRIL 7, 2013

CHAPTER FOUR

~ I believe in Jesus, who infused my life with his Spirit to make me smile ~

HERE I AM, LORD

It is helpful if at the beginning, when I enter the church, I can say: "Here I am, Lord. You love me and I am a sinner. Have mercy on us." Jesus tells us that if we do so, we return home forgiven; caressed by him, more loved by him in feeling this caress, this love. Thus, step by step, God transforms our heart with his mercy, and also transforms our life. We do not always stay the same, but are "formed." God shapes our heart; it is he, and we are molded like clay in the potter's hands; and God's love takes the place of our ego. This is why I think it is important to go to Church: not only to look at God, but to let ourselves be looked at by him. This is what I think.

ADDRESS,
JANUARY 4, 2018

OPEN YOUR HEART TO JESUS

Many times, in the face of a burden of life or a situation that saddens us, we try to talk about it with someone who listens to us, with a friend, with an expert.... This is a great thing to do, but let us not forget Jesus. Let us not forget to open ourselves to him and to recount our life to him, to entrust people and situations to him. Perhaps there are areas of our life that we have never opened up to him and which have remained dark, because they have never seen the Lord's light. Each of us has our own story. And if someone has this dark area, seek out Jesus; go to a missionary of mercy; go to a priest; go.... But go to Jesus, and tell Jesus about this.

ANGELUS,
JULY 9, 2017

ASK YOURSELF: DO I FEEL LOVED BY JESUS?

There is a dimension of the Christian experience, that perhaps we leave somewhat in the shadows: the spiritual and affective dimension. Feeling connected to the Lord by a special bond, as sheep to their shepherd. At times we rationalize faith too much and we run the risk of losing the perception of the timbre of that voice, of the voice of Jesus the Good Shepherd, which motivates and fascinates. This is what happened to the two disciples of Emmaus, whose hearts burned as the Risen One spoke along the way. It is the wondrous experience of feeling loved by Jesus. Ask yourselves the question: "Do I feel loved by Jesus? Do I feel loved by Jesus?" To him we are never strangers, but friends and brothers.

REGINA COELI,
MAY 7, 2017

JESUS IS WITH YOU

How often does Love have to ask us: "Why do you look for the living among the dead?" Our daily problems and worries can wrap us up in ourselves, in sadness and bitterness...and that is where death is. That is not the place to look for the One who is alive! Let the risen Jesus enter your life. Welcome him as a friend, with trust: he is life! If up till now you have kept him at a distance, step forward. He will receive you with open arms. If you have been indifferent, take a risk: you won't be disappointed. If following him seems difficult, don't be afraid. Trust him, be confident that he is close to you. He is with you, and he will give you the peace you are looking for and the strength to live as he would have you do.

HOMILY,
MARCH 30, 2013

GOD'S LOVE HAS A NAME AND A FACE

What is God's love? It is not something vague, some generic feeling. God's love has a name and a face: Jesus Christ, Jesus. Love for God is made manifest in Jesus. For we cannot love air.... Do we love air? Do we love all things? No, no we cannot; we love people and the person we love is Jesus, the gift of the Father among us. It is a love that gives value and beauty to everything else; a love that gives strength to the family, to work, to study, to friendship, to art, to all human activity. It even gives meaning to negative experiences, because this love allows us to move beyond these experiences, to go beyond them, not to remain prisoners of evil. It moves us beyond, always opening us to hope, that's it! Love of God in Jesus always opens us to hope, to that horizon of hope, to the final horizon of our pilgrimage. In this way our labors and failures find meaning. Even our sin finds meaning in the love of God because this love of God in Jesus Christ always forgives us. He loves us so much that he always forgives us.

ANGELUS,
AUGUST 11, 2013

LOVE INTRODUCES US TO KNOWLEDGE OF JESUS

Jesus says in today's Gospel: "He who has my commandments and keeps them, he it is who loves me; and he who loves me will be loved by my Father, and I will love him and manifest myself to him" (John 14:21). So, love introduces us to the knowledge of Jesus, thanks to the action of this "Advocate" that Jesus sent, that is, the Holy Spirit. Love for God and neighbor is the greatest commandment of the Gospel. The Lord today calls us to respond generously to the Gospel's call to love, placing God at the center of our lives and dedicating ourselves to the service of our brothers and sisters, especially those most in need of support and consolation.

REGINA COELI,
MAY 21, 2017

JESUS LIFTS THE ANGUISH FROM OUR HEART

Today Jesus says to each one: "Take courage; do not give in to life's burdens; do not close yourself off in the face of fears and sins. Come to me!"

He awaits us; he always awaits us. Not to magically resolve problems, but to strengthen us amid our problems. Jesus does not lift the burdens from our life, but the anguish from our heart; he does not take away our cross, but carries it with us. And with him every burden becomes light, because he is the comfort we seek.

ANGELUS,
JULY 9, 2017

UNSTOPPABLE LOVE

By the gift of his Spirit, Jesus enables us each to be signs of his wisdom, which triumphs over the wisdom of this world, and his mercy, which soothes even the most painful of injuries....

I encourage you to keep sharing with others the priceless wisdom that you have received, the love of God welling up in the heart of Jesus. Jesus wants to give this wisdom in abundance. He will surely crown your efforts to sow seeds of healing and reconciliation in your families, communities and the wider society of this nation. Does he not tell us that his wisdom is irresistible (cf. Luke 21:15)? His message of forgiveness and mercy uses a logic that not all will want to understand, and which will encounter obstacles. Yet his love, revealed on the cross, is ultimately unstoppable. It is like a spiritual GPS that unfailingly guides us toward the inner life of God and the heart of our neighbor.

HOMILY,
NOVEMBER 29, 2017

LOVE ONE ANOTHER AS I HAVE LOVED YOU

Today's Gospel—John Chapter 15—brings us back to the Last Supper, when we hear Jesus's new commandment. He says: "This is my commandment, that you love one another as I have loved you" (v. 12). Thinking of his imminent sacrifice on the cross, he adds: "Greater love has no man than this, that a man lay down his life for his friends. You are my friends, if you do what I command you" (v. 13–14). These words, said at the Last Supper, summarize Jesus's full message. Actually they summarize all that he did: Jesus gave his life for his friends. Friends who did not understand him, in fact they abandoned, betrayed and denied him at the crucial moment. This tells us that he loves us, even though we don't deserve his love. Jesus loves us in this way!

REGINA COELI,
MAY 10, 2015

LET US GO TO JESUS

When Jesus enters life, peace arrives, the kind that remains even in trials, in suffering. Let us go to Jesus; let us give him our time; let us encounter him each day in prayer, in a trusting and personal dialogue; let us become familiar with his Word; let us fearlessly rediscover his forgiveness; let us eat of his Bread of Life: we will feel loved; we will feel comforted by him.

It is he himself who asks it of us, almost insists on it. He repeats it again at the end of today's Gospel: "learn from me, and you will find rest for your life" (Matthew 11:29). And thus, let us learn to go to Jesus and, in the summer months, as we seek a little rest from what wearies the body, let us not forget to find true comfort in the Lord.

ANGELUS,
JULY 9, 2017

JESUS BRINGS THE TRANSFORMING LIFE OF GOD

Jesus is the incarnation of the Living God, the one who brings life amid so many deeds of death, such as sin, selfishness and self-absorption. Jesus accepts, loves, uplifts, encourages, forgives, restores the ability to walk, and gives back life. Throughout the Gospels we see how Jesus by his words and actions brings the transforming life of God. This was the experience of the woman who anointed the feet of the Lord with ointment: She felt understood, loved, and she responded by a gesture of love. She let herself be touched by God's mercy, she obtained forgiveness, and she started a new life. God, the Living One, is merciful.

HOMILY,
JUNE 16, 2013

THE POWER OF LOVING ATTENTION

Jesus's birth is our Heavenly Father's greatest gesture of love....

Jesus is God's gift to us and, if we welcome him, we too can become so to others—be a gift of God to others—first and foremost to those who have never experienced attention and tenderness. How many people in our life have never experienced a caress, loving attention, a kind gesture?

GENERAL AUDIENCE,
DECEMBER 27, 2017

JESUS TAKES ACTION

The power of Jesus confirms the authority of his teaching. He does not just speak with words, but he takes action. In this way, he manifests God's plan with words and with the power of his deeds. In the Gospel in fact, we see that in his earthly mission, Jesus reveals the love of God both through preaching and through countless gestures of attention and aid to the sick, the needy, children and sinners.

ANGELUS,
JANUARY 28, 2018

THE MIRACLE OF LOVE

Jesus is our mediator and he reconciles us, not only with the Father, but also among ourselves. He is the source of love who opens us to communion with our brothers and sisters, to love each other, removing all conflict and resentment. We know that resentment is bad; it causes a lot of pain and does us great harm! And Jesus removes all this and enables us to love one another. This is the miracle of Jesus. Let us ask Jesus, born for us, to help us adopt this twofold attitude of trust in the Father and love of neighbor. It is an attitude which transforms life and renders it more beautiful, more fruitful.

ANGELUS,
DECEMBER 26, 2017

LOVE ALWAYS KINDLES NEW LOVE

The love of Jesus Christ lasts forever, it has no end because it is the very life of God. This love conquers sin and gives the strength to rise and begin again, for through forgiveness the heart is renewed and rejuvenated. We all know it: our Father never tires of loving and his eyes never grow weary of watching the road to his home to see if the son who left and was lost is returning. We can speak of God's hope: our Father expects us always, he doesn't just leave the door open to us, but he awaits us. He is engaged in waiting for his children. And this Father also does not tire of loving the other son who, though staying at home with him the whole time, does not share in his mercy, in his compassion. God is not only at the origin of love, but in Jesus Christ he calls us to imitate his own way of loving: "As I have loved you, may you also love one another" (John 13:34). To the extent to which Christians live this love, they become credible disciples of Christ to the world. Love cannot bear being locked up in itself. By its nature it is open, it spreads and bears fruit, it always kindles new love.

HOMILY,
MARCH 28, 2014

THE WISDOM OF JESUS

Jesus did not teach us his wisdom by long speeches or by grand demonstrations of political or earthly power but by giving his life on the cross. Sometimes we can fall into the trap of believing in our own wisdom, but the truth is we can easily lose our sense of direction. At those times we need to remember that we have a sure compass before us, in the crucified Lord. In the cross, we find the wisdom that can guide our life with the light that comes from God.

In today's Gospel, the Lord tells us that, like him, we too may encounter rejection and obstacles, yet he will give us a wisdom that cannot be resisted (cf. Luke 21:15). He is speaking of the Holy Spirit, through whom the love of God has been poured into our hearts (cf. Romans 5:5).

HOMILY,
NOVEMBER 29, 2017

THE INEXHAUSTIBLE LOVE OF GOD

We are called to be more attentive, closer, to the needs of others. Like John the Baptist, in this way we can open the ways of hope in the desert of the barren hearts of many people.

"Every mountain and hill shall be made low" (40:4), Isaiah exhorts. The mountains and hills that must be made low are pride, arrogance, insolence. Where there is pride, where there is insolence, where there is arrogance, the Lord cannot enter because that heart is full of pride, of insolence, of arrogance. For this reason, we must allay this pride. We must take on attitudes of meekness and humility, without reproach, to listen, to speak with meekness and thus to prepare for the coming of our Savior, he who is meek and humble of heart (cf. Matthew 11:29)....

The Savior whom we await is able to transform our life with his grace, with the power of the Holy Spirit, with the power of love. The Holy Spirit, in fact, infuses our hearts with God's love, the inexhaustible source of purification, new life, and freedom.

ANGELUS,
DECEMBER 10, 2017

ACCEPT THE LOVE OF JESUS

To become holy we do not need to turn our eyes away and look somewhere else, or have as it were the face on a holy card! No, no, that is not necessary. To become saints only one thing is necessary: to accept the grace which the Father gives us in Jesus Christ. There, this grace changes our heart. We continue to be sinners for we are weak, but with this grace which makes us feel that the Lord is good, that the Lord is merciful, that the Lord waits for us, that the Lord pardons us, this immense grace that changes our heart.

ADDRESS,
JUNE 17, 2013

SAINTS AT HOME, SAINTS EVERYWHERE!

Many times, we are tempted to think that sainthood is reserved only to those who have the opportunity to break away from daily affairs in order to dedicate themselves exclusively to prayer. But it is not so!

Some think that sanctity is to close your eyes and to look like a holy icon. No! This is not sanctity! Sanctity is something greater, deeper, which God gives us. Indeed, it is precisely in living with love and offering one's own Christian witness in everyday affairs that we are called to become saints.

GENERAL AUDIENCE,
NOVEMBER 19, 2014

GOD MAKES ALL THINGS NEW

God is even now making all things new; the Holy Spirit is truly transforming us, and through us he also wants to transform the world in which we live. Let us open the doors to the Spirit, let us allow ourselves to be guided by him, and allow God's constant help to make us new men and women, inspired by the love of God which the Holy Spirit bestows on us! How beautiful it would be if each of you, every evening, could say: Today at school, at home, at work, guided by God, I showed a sign of love toward one of my friends, my parents, an older person! How beautiful!

HOMILY,
APRIL 28, 2013

THE HEART OF JESUS SPEAKS TO US

We do not believe in an ethereal God, we believe in a God who became flesh, who has a heart and this heart today speaks to us thus: "Come to me if you are tired, oppressed, and I will give you rest. But the smallest, treat them with compassion, with the same tenderness with which I treat you." The heart of Jesus Christ says this to us today.

HOMILY,
JUNE 12, 2015

GOD DRAWS US WITH TENDERNESS

God, who is in love with us, draws us to himself with his tenderness, by being born poor and frail in our midst, as one of us. He is born in Bethlehem, which means "house of bread." In this way, he seems to tell us that he is born as bread for us; he enters our life to give us his life; he comes into our world to give us his love. He does not come to devour or to lord it over us, but instead to feed and serve us. There is a straight line between the manger and the cross where Jesus will become bread that is broken. It is the straight line of love that gives and saves, the love that brings light to our lives and peace to our hearts.

HOMILY,
DECEMBER 24, 2016

EVERYTHING IS A GIFT OF LOVE

From the time we were small we are taught that it is not nice to boast. In my land, those who boast are called *pavoni* (peacocks). It is right, because boasting about what one is or what one has, apart from a certain arrogance, also reveals a lack of respect toward others, especially toward those who are less fortunate than we are. In this passage from the Letter to the Romans, however, the apostle Paul surprises us, as at least twice he exhorts us to boast. Of what, then, is it right to boast?...

Paul wants to make us understand that, if we learn to read everything in the light of the Holy Spirit, we realize that everything is grace! Everything is a gift! If we pay attention, in fact—in history, as in our life—it is not only we who are acting, but above all it is God. He is the absolute protagonist who creates everything as a gift of love, who weaves his plan of salvation and who leads it to fulfillment for us, through his Son Jesus.

GENERAL AUDIENCE,
FEBRUARY 15, 2017

PROCLAIM THE MESSAGE: "GOD IS LOVE!"

We are all called to witness and proclaim the message that "God is love," that God isn't far and insensitive to our human affairs. He is close to us, always beside us, walking with us to share our joys and our sorrows, our hopes and our struggles. He loves us very much and for that reason he became man, he came into the world not to condemn it, but so the world would be saved through Jesus (cf. John 3:16–17). And this is the love of God in Jesus, this love that is so difficult to understand but that we feel when we draw close to Jesus. And he always forgives us, he always awaits us, he loves us so much. And we feel the love of Jesus and the love of God.

ANGELUS,
JUNE 15, 2014

CHAPTER FIVE

~ I believe in the surprise of each day, in which love and strength will be manifest ~

GOD IS FULL OF SURPRISES

This is the surprising greatness of God, of a God who is full of surprises and who loves surprises: let us always keep alive the desire for and trust in God's surprises! It will help us to remember that we are constantly and primarily his children: not masters of our lives, but children of the Father; not autonomous and self-sufficient adults, but children who always need to be lifted up and embraced, who need love and forgiveness. Blessed are those Christian communities who live this authentic Gospel simplicity! Poor in means, they are rich in God. Blessed are the shepherds who do not ride the logic of worldly success, but follow the law of love: welcoming, listening, serving.

HOMILY,
OCTOBER 1, 2016

GOD "HAPPENS" IN EVERY SITUATION

"Do not be afraid…for he has been raised" (Matthew 28:5–6). Those words should affect our deepest convictions and certainties, the ways we judge and deal with the events of our daily lives, especially the ways we relate to others. The empty tomb should challenge us and rally our spirits. It should make us think, but above all it should encourage us to trust and believe that God "happens" in every situation and every person, and that his light can shine in the least expected and most hidden corners of our lives. He rose from the dead, from that place where nobody waits for anything, and now he waits for us—as he did the women—to enable us to share in his saving work. On this basis and with this strength, we Christians place our lives and our energy, our intelligence, our affections, and our will, at the service of discovering, and above all creating, paths of dignity.

HOMILY,
MARCH 31, 2018

GOD'S VISCERAL LOVE

"When Jesus saw the crowds..." (Matthew 5:1). In these first words of today's Gospel which we have just heard, we discover how Jesus wants to encounter us, the way that God always surprises his people (cf. Exodus 3:7). The first thing Jesus does is to look out and see the faces of his people. Those faces awaken God's visceral love. Jesus's heart was not moved by ideas or concepts, but by faces, persons. By life calling out for the life that the Father wants to give us.

HOMILY,
JANUARY 16, 2018

BECOME AMBASSADORS OF GOD'S LOVE

Jesus underscores two essential aspects for the life of a missionary disciple: the first, that his bond with Jesus is stronger than any other bond; the second, that the missionary brings not himself, but Jesus, and through him the love of the heavenly Father. These two aspects are connected, because the more Jesus is at the center of the heart and of the life of a disciple, the more this disciple is "transparent" to his presence. The two go hand in hand....

Those who allow themselves to be drawn into this bond of love and of life with the Lord Jesus become his representatives, his "ambassadors," above all in the way of being, of living.

ANGELUS,
JULY 2, 2017

HOW MANY TEARS DID YOU DRY TODAY?

The soul of a community is measured by how it manages to come together to face times of difficulty and adversity, in order to keep hope alive. By doing so, they give the greatest witness to the Gospel. The Lord tells us: "By this everyone will know that you are my disciples, if you have love for one another" (John 13:35). For faith opens us to a love that is concrete, not of ideas, but concrete, practical, generous, and compassionate, a love that can build and rebuild hope when it seems that all is lost. In this way, we share in God's own work, which the apostle John describes in showing us a God who wipes the tears of his children. God carries out this divine work with the same tender love that a mother has when she dries the tears of her children. What a beautiful question the Lord can ask each one of us at the end of the day: how many tears did you dry today?

HOMILY,
JANUARY 20, 2018

MAKE A HOME FOR EVERYONE!

St. Peter tells us that we are living stones, which form a spiritual edifice (cf. 1 Peter 2:5)…. Don't build a little chapel which holds only a small group of persons. Jesus asks us to make his living Church so large that it can hold all of humanity, that it can be a home for everyone!

PRAYER VIGIL,
WORLD YOUTH DAY, JULY 27, 2013

BECOME A REFLECTION OF GOD'S KINDNESS

The Bible readings for this Sunday, feast of the Most Holy Trinity, help us to enter into the identity of God. The second reading presents the departing words that St. Paul bids to the community of Corinth: "the grace of the Lord Jesus Christ and the love of God and the fellowship of the Holy Spirit be with all of you" (2 Corinthians 13:13). This—as we say—"blessing" of the apostle is the fruit of his personal experience with God's love, that love which the Risen Christ revealed to him, which transformed his life and "impelled" him to take the Gospel to the peoples. Beginning from his experience of grace, Paul could exhort Christians with these words: "Rejoice. Mend your ways, encourage one another, agree with one another" (v. 11). The Christian community, even with all its human limitations, can become a reflection of the communion of the Trinity, of its kindness, of its beauty.

ANGELUS,
JUNE 11, 2017

INVEST IN LOVE

In the poor, Jesus knocks on the doors of our heart, thirsting for our love.... To love the poor means to combat all forms of poverty, spiritual and material.

And it will also do us good. Drawing near to the poor in our midst will touch our lives. It will remind us of what really counts: to love God and our neighbor. Only this lasts forever, everything else passes away. What we invest in love remains, the rest vanishes.

HOMILY,
NOVEMBER 19, 2017

ONLY LOVE GIVES MEANING AND HAPPINESS TO LIFE

Jesus reminds us that his way is the way of love, and that there is no true love without self-sacrifice. We are called to not let ourselves be absorbed by the vision of this world, but to be ever more aware of the need and of the effort for we Christians to walk against the current and uphill.

Jesus completes his proposal with words that express a great and ever valid wisdom, because they challenge the egocentric mentality and behavior. He exhorts: "Whoever would save his life will lose it, and whoever loses his life for my sake will find it" (Matthew 16:25). This paradox contains the golden rule that God inscribed in human nature created in Christ: the rule that only love gives meaning and happiness to life. To spend one's own talents, one's energy and one's time only to save, protect and fulfill oneself, in reality leads to losing oneself, that is, to a sad and barren existence. Instead let us live for the Lord and base our life on love, as Jesus did: We will be able to savor authentic joy, and our life will not be barren; it will be fruitful.

ANGELUS,
SEPTEMBER 3, 2017

RESPOND TO EVIL WITH GOOD

True happiness is being with the Lord and living for love. Do you believe this? True happiness is not in having something or in becoming someone; true happiness is being with the Lord and living for love. Do you believe this? We must go forth, believing in this. So, the ingredients for a happy life are called Beatitudes: blessed are the simple, the humble who make room for God, who are able to weep for others and for their own mistakes, who remain meek, fight for justice, are merciful to all, safeguard purity of heart, always work for peace and abide in joy, do not hate and, even when suffering, respond to evil with good.

ANGELUS,
NOVEMBER 1, 2017

CONTINUE THE MISSION OF THE GOOD SAMARITAN

The world vitally needs the Gospel of Jesus Christ. Through the Church, Christ continues his mission as the Good Samaritan, caring for the bleeding wounds of humanity, and as Good Shepherd, constantly seeking out those who wander along winding paths that lead nowhere. Thank God, many significant experiences continue to testify to the transformative power of the Gospel. I think of the gesture of the Dinka student who, at the cost of his own life, protected a student from the enemy Nuer tribe. I think of that Eucharistic celebration in Kitgum, in northern Uganda, where, after brutal massacres by a rebel group, a missionary made the people repeat the words of Jesus on the cross: "My God, My God, why have you abandoned me?" as an expression of the desperate cry of the brothers and sisters of the crucified Lord. For the people, that celebration was an immense source of consolation and courage. We can think too of countless testimonies to how the Gospel helps to overcome narrowness, conflict, racism, tribalism, and to promote everywhere, and among all, reconciliation, fraternity, and sharing.

MESSAGE FOR WORLD MISSION DAY,
JUNE 4, 2017

THE LOVING CLOSENESS OF GOD TO ALL

Today the Gospel presents the Holy Family to us on the sorrowful road of exile, seeking refuge in Egypt. Joseph, Mary, and Jesus experienced the tragic fate of refugees, which is marked by fear, uncertainty and unease (cf. Matthew 2:13–15, 19–23). Unfortunately, in our own time, millions of families can identify with this sad reality. Almost every day the television and papers carry news of refugees fleeing from hunger, war, and other grave dangers, in search of security and a dignified life for themselves and for their families.

Jesus wanted to belong to a family who experienced these hardships, so that no one would feel excluded from the loving closeness of God. The flight into Egypt caused by Herod's threat shows us that God is present where man is in danger, where man is suffering, where he is fleeing, where he experiences rejection and abandonment.

ANGELUS,
DECEMBER 29, 2013

NO ONE BELONGS ON THE FRINGES

Jesus does not ask his Father that all may be equal, identical, for unity is not meant to neutralize or silence differences. Unity is not an idol or the result of forced integration; it is not a harmony bought at the price of leaving some people on the fringes. The richness of a land is born precisely from the desire of each of its parts to share its wisdom with others. Unity can never be a stifling uniformity imposed by the powerful, or a segregation that does not value the goodness of others. The unity sought and offered by Jesus acknowledges what each people and each culture are called to contribute to this land of blessings. Unity is a reconciled diversity, for it will not allow personal or community wrongs to be perpetrated in its name. We need the riches that each people has to offer, and we must abandon the notion that there are superior or inferior cultures.

HOMILY,
JANUARY 17, 2018

WE MUST OFFER CHRISTIAN HOPE

He gives us grace freely, he freely gives it to us, and we must give it freely to our brothers and sisters....

In the midst of so many sufferings, so many problems, there are people who live without hope. Each one of us can think in silence of people who live with no hope and are steeped in profound sadness from which they struggle to emerge, believing they have found happiness in alcohol, in drugs, in gambling, in the power of money, in sexuality unbridled by rules.... However, they find themselves even more disappointed and sometimes vent their rage against life with violent behavior unworthy of the human being.

How many sad people, how many sad people without hope! Think too of the many young people who after trying out so many things, fail to find a meaning for life and opt for suicide as a solution. Do you know how many young people commit suicide in the world today? A large number. Why? They have no hope. They have tried so many things and society, which is cruel—it is cruel!—cannot give you hope. Hope is like grace: it cannot be bought, it is a gift of God. We must offer Christian hope with our witness, our freedom, and our joy.

ADDRESS,
JUNE 17, 2013

TAKE CARE OF THE WEAKEST

The Easter of Christ raised something else in the world: the novelty of dialogue and of a relationship, something new that has become a responsibility for Christians. In fact, Jesus said: "From this everyone will know that you are my disciples: if you have love for one another" (John 13:35). This is why we cannot confine ourselves to our private groups, but we are called to take care of the common good, to take care of our brothers, especially the weakest and most marginalized. Only fraternity can guarantee lasting peace, can defeat poverty, can extinguish tensions and wars, can eradicate corruption and crime.

REGINA COELI,
APRIL 2, 2018

STEP OUT BRAVELY

Christians must be brave. In facing a problem, in facing a social or religious crisis, they must have the courage to move onwards, to go ahead bravely. And when nothing can be done, patiently putting up with it. Tolerating. Courage and patience, these two virtues of Paul. Courage: moving ahead, bearing a forceful witness: onward! Putting up with things: bearing on our shoulders the things that cannot yet be changed. But moving forward with this patience, with this patience that grace gives us.

However, what must we do with courage and with patience? Come out of ourselves, step out of ourselves. Go out of our communities to go where men and women live in order to work and suffer and proclaim to them the mercy of the Father who made men and women acquainted with him in Jesus Christ of Nazareth. Proclaim this grace that was given to us by Jesus.

If I asked priests on Holy Thursday to be shepherds with the smell of their sheep, I say to you, dear brothers and sisters: be everywhere heralds of the word of life in our neighborhoods, our workplaces, and everywhere that people meet one another and develop relationships. You must go outside. I do not understand Christian communities that are shut into a parish.

ADDRESS,
JUNE 17, 2013

BRING LOVE AND PEACE TO ALL

Some people ask how it is possible to speak of good news when so many people around us are suffering. Where is the good news when so much injustice, poverty, and misery cast a shadow over us and our world? But I want a very clear message to go out from this place. I want people to know that you, the young men and women of Myanmar, are not afraid to believe in the good news of God's mercy, because it has a name and a face: Jesus Christ. As messengers of this good news, you are ready to bring a word of hope to the Church, to your own country, and to the wider world. You are ready to bring good news for your suffering brothers and sisters who need your prayers and your solidarity, but also your enthusiasm for human rights, for justice, and for the growth of that "love and peace" which Jesus brings.

HOMILY,
NOVEMBER 30, 2017

BE CLOSE TO THOSE IN DISTRESS

My thoughts go to those suffering from HIV/AIDS, and particularly to the orphaned children and parents left without love and support as a result of this illness. Continue to be close to those in distress, to the sick, and especially to the children. I ask you, particularly, to offer my gratitude to the many men and women who present Christ's tenderness and love in Catholic healthcare institutions. The service which the Church offers to the sick, through pastoral care, prayer, clinics, and hospices, must always find its source and model in Christ, who loved us and gave himself up for us (cf. Galatians 2:20). Indeed, how else could we be followers of the Lord if we did not personally engage in ministry to the sick, the poor, the dying, and the destitute?

ADDRESS TO BISHOPS,
NOVEMBER 6, 2014

RECOGNIZE THE DIGNITY OF EVERY HUMAN BEING

If I encounter a person sleeping outdoors on a cold night, I can view him or her as an annoyance, an idler, an obstacle in my path, a troubling sight, a problem for politicians to sort out, or even a piece of refuse cluttering a public space. Or I can respond with faith and charity, and see in this person a human being with a dignity identical to my own, a creature infinitely loved by the Father, an image of God, a brother or sister redeemed by Jesus Christ. That is what it is to be a Christian! Can holiness somehow be understood apart from this lively recognition of the dignity of each human being?

GAUDETE ET EXSULTATE, 98

SERVE OTHERS WITH LOVE

Love is service. It is serving others. When after the washing of the feet Jesus explained the gesture to the apostles, he taught that we are made to serve one another, and if I say that I love but I don't serve the other, don't help the other, don't enable him to go forward, don't sacrifice myself for him, this isn't love. You have carried the cross [the World Youth Day cross]: there is the sign of love. That history of God's love involved in works and dialogue, with respect, with forgiveness, with patience during so many centuries of history with his people, ends there—his Son on the cross, the greatest service, which is giving one's life, sacrificing oneself, helping others.

ADDRESS TO CHILDREN AND YOUNG PEOPLE,
JUNE 21, 2015

LOVE IS A DEED, NOT A WORD

Love, therefore, is the practical service that we offer to others. Love is not a word, it is a deed, a service; humble service, hidden and silent, like Jesus said himself: "do not let your left hand know what your right hand is doing" (Matthew 6:3). It entails putting at others' disposal the gifts that the Holy Spirit has given us, so that the community might thrive (cf. 1 Corinthians 12:4–11). Furthermore, it is expressed in the sharing of material goods, so that no one be left in need. This sharing with and dedication to those in need is the lifestyle that God suggests, even to non-Christians, as the authentic path of humanity....

When you can forget yourself and think of others, this is love!

JUBILEE AUDIENCE,
MARCH 12, 2016

LOVE IS IN THE DETAILS

Let us not forget that Jesus asked his disciples to pay attention to details.

The little detail that wine was running out at a party.

The little detail that one sheep was missing.

The little detail of noticing the widow who offered her two small coins.

The little detail of having spare oil for the lamps, should the bridegroom delay.

The little detail of asking the disciples how many loaves of bread they had.

The little detail of having a fire burning and a fish cooking as he waited for the disciples at daybreak.

A community that cherishes the little details of love, whose members care for one another and create an open and evangelizing environment, is a place where the risen Lord is present, sanctifying it in accordance with the Father's plan. There are times when, by a gift of the Lord's love, we are granted, amid these little details, consoling experiences of God.

GAUDETE ET EXSULTATE, 144–145

ACTIONS GREAT AND SMALL

It is precisely Christ's love that the Holy Spirit pours into our hearts to make everyday wonders in the Church and in the world. There are many small and great actions which obey the Lord's commandment: "Love one another as I have loved you" (cf. John 15:12). Small everyday actions, actions of closeness to an elderly person, to a child, to a sick person, to a lonely person, those in difficulty, without a home, without work, an immigrant, a refugee.... Thanks to the strength of the Word of Christ, each one of us can make ourselves the brother or sister of those whom we encounter. Actions of closeness, actions which manifest the love that Christ taught us.

REGINA COELI,
MAY 10, 2015

WHATEVER YOU DID FOR THE LEAST OF THESE

To those of you who housed and fed people seeking safety—in churches, convents, and rectories—and who continue to assist those still struggling, I thank you. You are a credit to the Church. You are the pride of your nation. I personally thank each one of you. For whatever you did for the least of Christ's brothers and sisters, you did for him (cf. Matthew 25:41).

HOMILY,
JANUARY 17, 2015

CHAPTER SIX

~ I believe in my life story, and in the eternal kingdom of life ~

EACH OF US IS A CHERISHED STORY

Our life is not pure chance or a mere struggle for survival, rather each of us is a cherished story loved by God. That we have "found grace in his eyes" means that the Creator sees a unique beauty in our being and that he has a magnificent plan for our lives. The awareness of this certainty, of course, does not resolve all our problems nor does it take away life's uncertainties. But it does have the power to transform our life deeply.

MESSAGE TO YOUTH,
FEBRUARY 11, 2018

THE MOST BEAUTIFUL PLACE THAT EXISTS

Paradise is not a fairytale place, much less an enchanted garden. Paradise is the embrace of God, infinite Love, and we enter there thanks to Jesus, who died on the cross for us. Where there is Jesus there is mercy and happiness; without him there is cold and darkness. At the hour of death, a Christian repeats to Jesus: "Remember me." And even if there may no longer be anyone who remembers us, Jesus is there, beside us. He wants to take us to the most beautiful place that exists. He wants to take us there with the small or great deal of good that we have done in our life, so that nothing of what he has already redeemed may be lost. And into the Father's house he will also bring everything in us that still needs redemption: the shortcomings and mistakes of an entire life. This is the aim of our existence: that all be fulfilled, and be transformed into love.

GENERAL AUDIENCE,
OCTOBER 25, 2017

THE LORD WILL DRY EVERY TEAR

In the book of the prophet Jeremiah, chapters 30 and 31 are called the "Book of Consolation," because God's mercy is presented with his great capacity to comfort and open to hope the heart of the afflicted.... God is near, and he does great works of salvation for those who trust in him. One must not succumb to desperation, but continue to be certain that good conquers evil and that the Lord will dry every tear and free us from all fear.

Thus Jeremiah lends his voice to God's words of love for his people: "I have loved you with a love everlasting; therefore I have continued my faithfulness to you. Again I will build you, and you shall be built, O virgin Israel! Again you shall adorn yourself with timbrels, and shall go forth in the dance of the merrymakers" (31:3–4). The Lord is faithful, he does not leave one to despair. God loves with boundless love, which not even sin can restrain, and thanks to him the heart of man is filled with joy and consolation.

GENERAL AUDIENCE,
MARCH 16, 2016

NOT WHAT WE HAVE, BUT WHAT WE GIVE

Today we might ask ourselves: "What counts for me in life? Where am I making my investments?" In fleeting riches, with which the world is never satisfied, or in the wealth bestowed by God, who gives eternal life? This is the choice before us: to live in order to gain things on earth, or to give things away in order to gain heaven. Where heaven is concerned, what matters is not what we have, but what we give, for "those who store up treasures for themselves, do not grow rich in the sight of God" (Luke 12:21).

HOMILY,
NOVEMBER 19, 2017

WE WILL BE JUDGED ON LOVE

Jesus reveals the decisive criterion of his judgment, namely, concrete love for a neighbor in difficulty. And in this way the power of love, the kingship of God is revealed: in solidarity with those who suffer in order to engender everywhere compassion and works of mercy....

At the end of our life we will be judged on love, that is, on our concrete commitment to love and serve Jesus in our littlest and neediest brothers and sisters. That mendicant, that needy person who reaches out his hand is Jesus; that sick person whom I must visit is Jesus; that inmate is Jesus, that hungry person is Jesus. Let us consider this.

ANGELUS,
NOVEMBER 26, 2017

OUR PASSPORT TO PARADISE

In the poor, Jesus knocks on the doors of our heart, thirsting for our love. When we overcome our indifference and, in the name of Jesus, we give of ourselves for the least of his brethren, we are his good and faithful friends, with whom he loves to dwell. God greatly appreciates the attitude described in today's first reading: that of the "good wife" who "opens her hand to the poor, and reaches out her hands to the needy" (Proverbs 31:10, 20). Here we see true goodness and strength: not in closed fists and crossed arms, but in ready hands outstretched to the poor, to the wounded flesh of the Lord.

There, in the poor, we find the presence of Jesus, who, though rich, became poor (cf. 2 Corinthians 8:9). For this reason, in them, in their weakness, a "saving power" is present. And if in the eyes of the world they have little value, they are the ones who open to us the way to heaven; they are our "passport to paradise."

HOMILY,
NOVEMBER 19, 2017

WE WERE MADE FOR ETERNAL LIFE

Wherever we go, we are called as Christians to proclaim the liberating news that forgiveness for sins committed is possible, that God is greater than our sinfulness, that he freely loves us at all times and that we were made for communion and eternal life. The Lord asks us to be joyous heralds of this message of mercy and hope! It is thrilling to experience the joy of spreading this good news, sharing the treasure entrusted to us, consoling broken hearts, and offering hope to our brothers and sisters experiencing darkness.

LENTEN MESSAGE,
DECEMBER 26, 2013

DO NOT FEAR, I AM WITH YOU

In today's Gospel (cf. Matthew 10:26–33) the Lord Jesus, after having called and sent the disciples on mission, teaches them, and prepares them to face the trials and persecutions they will have to endure....

But in all this, the Lord continues to tell us, as he did to the disciples of his time: "Do not fear!" Let us not forget these words: always, when we experience any tribulation, any persecution, anything that causes us to suffer, let us listen to the voice of Jesus in our hearts: "Do not fear! Do not fear! Go Forth! I am with you!" Do not fear those who mock you and mistreat you and do not fear those who ignore you or respect you "to your face," but fight the Gospel "behind your back." There are so many who smile to our face, but fight the Gospel behind our backs. We all know them. Jesus does not leave us all alone, because we are precious to him. That is why he does not leave us all alone. Each one of us is precious to Jesus and he accompanies us.

ANGELUS,
JUNE 25, 2017

GOD BELIEVES IN US

As soon as we give God the chance, he remembers us. He is ready to completely and forever cancel our sin, because his memory—unlike our own—does not record evil that has been done or keep score of injustices experienced. God has no memory of sin, but only of us, of each of us, we who are his beloved children. And he believes that it is always possible to start anew, to raise ourselves up.

Let us also ask for the gift of this open and living memory. Let us ask for the grace of never closing the doors of reconciliation and pardon, but rather of knowing how to go beyond evil and differences, opening every possible pathway of hope. As God believes in us, infinitely beyond any merits we have, so too we are called to instill hope and provide opportunities to others. Because even if the Holy Door closes, the true door of mercy which is the heart of Christ always remains open wide for us. From the lacerated side of the Risen One until the very end of time flow mercy, consolation, and hope.

HOMILY,
NOVEMBER 20, 2016

WHAT IS ETERNAL LIFE?

"God so loved the world that he gave his only Son, so that everyone who believes in him might not perish but might have eternal life" (John 3:16). What is this eternal life? It is the immeasurable and freely given love of the Father which Jesus gave on the cross, offering his life for our salvation. And this love with the action of the Holy Spirit has shined a new light on the earth and into every human heart that welcomes him; a light that reveals the dark corners, the hardships that impede us from bearing the good fruits of charity and of mercy.

ANGELUS,
JUNE 11, 2017

JESUS OPENS THE GATES TO PARADISE

The humiliation of Jesus reaches its utmost in the Passion: he is sold for thirty pieces of silver and betrayed by the kiss of a disciple whom he had chosen and called his friend....

And so the hour of death on the cross arrives, that most painful form of shame reserved for traitors, slaves, and the worst kind of criminals. But isolation, defamation, and pain are not yet the full extent of his deprivation. To be totally in solidarity with us, he also experiences on the cross the mysterious abandonment of the Father. In his abandonment, however, he prays and entrusts himself: "Father, into your hands I commit my spirit" (Luke 23:46). Hanging from the wood of the cross, besides derision he now confronts the last temptation: to come down from the cross, to conquer evil by might, and to show the face of a powerful and invincible God.

Jesus, however, even here at the height of his annihilation, reveals the true face of God, which is mercy. He forgives those who are crucifying him, he opens the gates of paradise to the repentant thief and he touches the heart of the centurion. If the mystery of evil is unfathomable, then the reality of Love poured out through him is infinite, reaching even to the tomb and to hell. He takes upon himself all our pain that he may redeem it, bringing light to darkness, life to death, love to hatred.

HOMILY,
MARCH 20, 2016

LOVE NEVER ENDS

Those who have met Jesus no longer fear anything. We too can repeat the words of the elderly Simeon; he too was blessed by the encounter with Christ, after a lifetime spent in anticipation of this event: "Lord, now let your servant depart in peace, according to your word; for my eyes have seen your salvation" (Luke 2:29–30). At that instant, at last, we will no longer need anything; we will no longer see in a confused way. We will no longer weep in vain, because all has passed; even the prophecies, even consciousness. But not love: this endures. Because "love never ends" (1 Corinthians 13:8).

GENERAL AUDIENCE,
OCTOBER 25, 2017

WAITING FOR A NEW CREATION

If we pay attention, around us everything is groaning: Creation itself groans; we human beings groan and the Holy Spirit groans within us, in our heart. Now, these groans are not a barren, disconsolate lament, but—as the apostle explains—they are the groaning of a woman in labor; they are the groans of those who suffer, but know that a new life is about to be born. And in our case, it is truly so. We are still gripped by the consequences of our sin and everything around us, still bears the sign of our weariness, of our shortcomings, of our closure. At the same time, however, we know we have been saved by the Lord and that we have already been able to contemplate and to foretaste, in ourselves and in what surrounds us, the signs of the Resurrection, of Easter, which brings about a new creation.

This is the content of our hope. The Christian does not live outside of the world; he knows how to recognize in his life and in what surrounds him the signs of evil, of selfishness, and of sin. He is in solidarity with those who suffer, with those who weep, with those who are marginalized, with those who despair.... However, at the same time, the Christian has learned to read all of this with the eyes of Easter, with the eyes of the Risen Christ. Thus, he knows that we are living in the time of waiting, the time of longing which transcends the present, the time of fulfillment. In hope we know that the Lord wants to definitively heal with his mercy the wounded and humiliated hearts and all that man has spoiled by his impiety, and that in this way, He regenerates a new world and a new humanity, finally reconciling them in his love.

GENERAL AUDIENCE,
FEBRUARY 22, 2017

A NEW HEAVEN AND A NEW EARTH

How often are we Christians tempted to give in to disappointment, to pessimism.... At times we allow ourselves to resort to pointless complaining, or we remain speechless and do not even know what to ask for, what to hope for.... Yet once more, however, the Holy Spirit—the breath of our hope, who keeps the groans and the expectation alive in our heart—comes to help us. The Spirit sees for us beyond the negative semblance of the present; he already reveals to us the new heavens and the new earth that the Lord is preparing for mankind.

GENERAL AUDIENCE,
FEBRUARY 22, 2017

JESUS HAS GIVEN US ETERNAL LIFE

God never gives in to the possibility that a person could stay estranged from his love, provided, however, that he find in him or her some sign of repentance for the evil done.

By our efforts alone, we cannot be reconciled to God. Sin truly is the expression of the rejection of his love, with the consequence of closing in on ourselves, deluding ourselves into thinking that we have found greater freedom and autonomy.... However, Jesus comes to find us like a good shepherd who is not content until he has found the lost sheep, as we read in the Gospel (cf. Luke 15:4–6). He rebuilds the bridge that connects us to the Father and allows us to rediscover our dignity as children. By the offering of his life he has reconciled us to the Father and given us eternal life (cf. John 10:15).

JUBILEE AUDIENCE,
APRIL 30, 2016

EVERYTHING WILL BE SAVED

Christians are not made for boredom; if anything, for patience. We know that hidden in the monotony of certain identical days is a mystery of grace. There are people who with the perseverance of their love become as wells that irrigate the desert. Nothing happens in vain; and no situation in which a Christian finds himself is completely resistant to love. No night is so long as to make us forget the joy of the sunrise. And the darker the night, the closer the dawn. If we remain united with Jesus, the cold of difficult moments does not paralyze us; and if even the whole world preached against hope, if it said that the future would bring only dark clouds, a Christian knows that in that same future there will be Christ's return. No one knows when this will take place, but the thought that at the end of our history there will be Merciful Jesus suffices in order to have faith and not to curse life. Everything will be saved. Everything. We will suffer; there will be moments that give rise to anger and indignation, but the sweet and powerful memory of Christ will drive away the temptation to think that this life is a mistake.

GENERAL AUDIENCE,
OCTOBER 11, 2017

NOTHING CAN SEPARATE US FROM THE LOVE OF CHRIST

We have listened to the words of St Paul: "For I am sure that neither death, nor life, nor angels, nor principalities, nor things present, nor things to come, nor powers, nor height, nor depth, nor anything else in all creation, will be able to separate us from the love of God in Christ Jesus our Lord" (Romans 8:38–39).

The apostle presents the love of God as the deepest and most compelling reason for Christian trust and hope. He lists the opposing and mysterious forces that can threaten the journey of faith. But immediately he states with confidence that even if our entire life is surrounded by threats, nothing will ever be able to separate us from the love which Christ himself has obtained for us by his total self-gift. Even the demonic powers, which are hostile to man, stand powerless before the intimate union of love that exists between Jesus and whoever receives him in faith.

HOMILY,
NOVEMBER 4, 2013

BE RENEWED BY GOD'S SPIRIT

You too need to see the entirety of your life as a mission. Try to do so by listening to God in prayer and recognizing the signs that he gives you. Always ask the Spirit what Jesus expects from you at every moment of your life and in every decision you must make, so as to discern its place in the mission you have received. Allow the Spirit to forge in you the personal mystery that can reflect Jesus Christ in today's world.

May you come to realize what that word is, the message of Jesus that God wants to speak to the world by your life. Let yourself be transformed. Let yourself be renewed by the Spirit, so that this can happen, lest you fail in your precious mission. The Lord will bring it to fulfillment despite your mistakes and missteps, provided that you do not abandon the path of love but remain ever open to his supernatural grace, which purifies and enlightens.

GAUDETE ET EXSULTATE, 23–24

PREPARE FOR THE WEDDING FEAST

Our celebration of Mass teaches us to be "Eucharistic" men and women, conformed ever more fully to Christ in our thoughts, words, and actions. After Mass, the Lord continues his Real Presence among us in the Blessed Sacrament, as a reminder that the fruits of the Eucharist are meant to expand daily through our growth in holiness, in union with the Church, and in loving service to our brothers and sisters, especially those in need. May our regular celebration of the Eucharistic banquet strengthen us in our journey of faith, until at last we share eternally in the unending joy of the wedding feast of the Lamb.

GENERAL AUDIENCE,
APRIL 4, 2018

AN INVITATION TO YOU AND TO ME

To celebrate Easter is to believe once more that God constantly breaks into our personal histories, challenging our "conventions," those fixed ways of thinking and acting that end up paralyzing us. To celebrate Easter is to allow Jesus to triumph over the craven fear that so often assails us and tries to bury every kind of hope.

The stone before the tomb shared in this, the women of the Gospel shared in this, and now the invitation is addressed once more to you and to me. An invitation to break out of our routines and to renew our lives, our decisions, and our existence. An invitation that must be directed to where we stand, what we are doing, and what we are, with the "power ratio" that is ours. Do we want to share in this message of life or do we prefer simply to continue standing speechless before events as they happen?

He is not here…he is raised! And he awaits you in Galilee. He invites you to go back to the time and place of your first love and he says to you: Do not be afraid, follow me.

HOMILY,
MARCH 31, 2018

Shortly before his thirty-third birthday and his ordination as a Jesuit priest, which took place on December 13, 1969, Jorge Bergoglio made an eight-day retreat and penned this heartfelt credo.

"I Believe"

Personal credo of Jorge Mario Bergoglio

I want to believe in God the Father who loves me like a child, and in Jesus, the Lord who infused my life with His Spirit, to make me smile and so carry me to the eternal Kingdom of life.

I believe in the Church.

I believe in my life story, which was pierced by God's loving gaze, who on that spring day of 21st September, came out to meet me to invite me to follow him.

I believe in my pain, made fruitless by the egotism in which I take refuge.

I believe in the stinginess of my soul, which seeks to take without giving.

I believe in the goodness of others, and that I must love them without fear and without betraying them, never seeking my own security.

I believe in the religious life.

I believe I wish to love a lot.

I believe in the burning death of each day, from which I flee but which smiles at me, inviting me to accept her.

I believe in God's patience, as good and as welcoming as a summer's night.

I believe that Dad is with the Lord in heaven.

I believe that Fr. Duarte is there, too, interceding for my priesthood.

I believe in Mary, my Mother, who loves me and will never leave me alone.

And I believe in the surprise of each day, in which will be manifest love, strength, betrayal, and sin, which will be always with me until that definitive encounter with that marvelous face which I do not know, which always escapes me, but which I wish to know and love. Amen.

About the Author

Pope Francis, formerly Cardinal Jorge Mario Bergoglio, SJ, served the Jesuits as novice master, lecturer, provincial, confessor, and spiritual director before Pope John Paul II named him Archbishop of Buenos Aires. He was elected to the papacy on March 13, 2013. He is the first pope from the Americas and the first pope to choose the name Francis, in honor of St. Francis of Assisi.

~~~

About the Editor

Alicia (Ramírez de Arellano) von Stamwitz was born in Cuba and immigrated to the United States in 1960. She is an award-winning freelance author and longtime editor with the religious press. Her interviews and profiles of today's most influential spiritual leaders are published internationally. She lives in Missouri with her family. More information can be found at www.aliciavonstamwitz.com.
~~~